Dear Mom,

Thank You For Being Mine

Books by Scott Matthews and Tamara Nikuradse

Dear Mom, Thank You for Being Mine

Dear Dad, Thank You for Being Mine

Stuck in the Seventies
(with Jay Kerness, Jay Steele, and Greg White)

Dear Mom,

Thank You for Being Mine

Scott Matthews
Tamara Nikuradse

BANTAM BOOKS   *New York*   *Toronto*   *London*   *Sydney*   *Auckland*

DEAR MOM, THANK YOU FOR BEING MINE

A Bantam Book / May 1993

All rights reserved.
Copyright © 1993 by Scott Matthews and Tamara Nikuradse.
Book design by Ellen Cipriano
No part of this book may be reproduced or transmitted in any form or by any means, electronic
or mechanical, including photocopying, recording, or by any information storage and retrieval system,
without permission in writing from the publisher.
For information address: Bantam Books.

Library of Congress Cataloging-in-Publication Data
Matthews, Scott.
   Dear Mom, thank you for being mine / by Scott Matthews, Tamara
Nikuradse.
      p.   cm.
   ISBN 0-553-37197-5
   1. Mother and child—Miscellanea.   2. Gratitude—Miscellanea.
   I. Nikuradse, Tamara.   II. Title.
HQ759.M393   1993
306.874'3—dc20   92-41689
                                                              CIP

Published simultaneously in the United States and Canada

PRINTED IN THE UNITED STATES OF AMERICA

FFG 0 9 8 7 6 5 4 3 2 1

*Dedicated to all Moms who
make these thank-yous possible*

Acknowledgments

Thank you to our parents, Glenn and Gail Matthews and Charles and Odeline Townes, for the inspiration to write this book.

Thank you to our friends who helped make this book possible: Len Berardis, Susan and Michael Caplan, Evelyn Fazio, Joline Godfrey, Sheila Kenyon, Brett and Ginger Matthews, Becky and Rachel Salmon, Tanya Townes, Connie Patsalos and Cheryl Wells (for the jump start), and the three coauthors of our first book, *Stuck in the Seventies*, Jay Kerness, Jay Steele, and Greg White.

Thank you, Mary Jane Ross, our agent, for your diligence and guidance.

Thank you, Barbara Alpert, our friend and editor, for your enthusiasm, encouragement, and editing prowess. Thank you, Matthew Shear, for your confidence. And thank you to all of Scott's friends and colleagues at Bantam who brought this book to you.

Thank you.

Scott and Tamara

Introduction

During a recent move, we came across a box full of family pictures. You know the ones. Pictures celebrating first potties and first steps, first dances and first dates. Pictures of bare baby bottoms on fur rugs and geeky grins found only in high school yearbooks.

With each picture the memories started to flood, and they reminded us of all the things that our parents have given to us—material and immaterial—things that we still carry with us to this day, things that made us who we are today. The pictures also reminded us of the many times that we forgot to thank our parents, especially for the little things that we had taken for granted. Deciding that it was never too late, we started compiling our thank-yous to present to our parents as long-overdue gifts.

P.S. We know that every child has some special thank-yous to say to his or her parents, so we left room for you to add your own thoughts at the end. Of course, feel free to edit anything in here to make it fit your mother perfectly.

Dear Mom,

Thank you . . .

Thank you for creating me with love.

Thank you for talking to me and keeping me company while I was in the oven.

Thank you for not striking me back when I kicked you in the ribs.

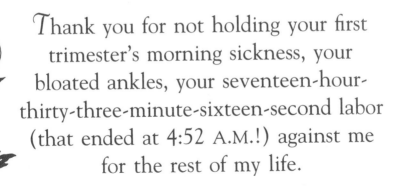

Thank you for satisfying my cravings for an anchovy-and-dill-pickle hot fudge sundae.

Thank you for not holding your first trimester's morning sickness, your bloated ankles, your seventeen-hour-thirty-three-minute-sixteen-second labor (that ended at 4:52 A.M.!) against me for the rest of my life.

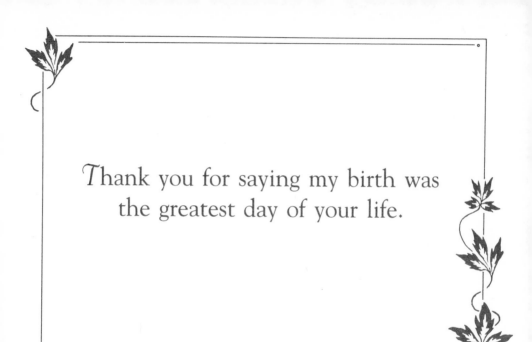

Thank you for saying my birth was
the greatest day of your life.

Thank you for asking the doctor to
spank me lightly.

Thank you for instructing the doctor to
give me an innie instead of an outie.

Thank you for decorating my room with
bright colors and a mobile
over my crib.

Thank you for flattening my ears when I lay on my tummy.

Thank you for blowing wet kisses on my stomach.

Thank you for rocking my cradle.

Thank you for saying "Mama . . . Mama . . . Mama" one zillion times until I finally caught on.

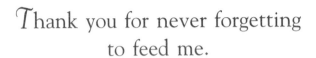

Thank you for never forgetting
to feed me.

Thank you for testing every baby food
flavor ever made to figure out which
one I liked the best.

Thank you for picking up my spoon or
bowl twelve times per feeding.

Thank you for coaxing the tunnel to open by going "Choo-choo-choo."

Thank you for cleaning up the mess when the choo-choo train backed up and spit up all over you.

Thank you for praising my "burpsidoodles."

Thank you for changing my
diapers—often.

Thank you for soothing those nasty
rashes with baby powder.

Thank you for potty training me and
for being so proud when I got it right.

Thank you for playing This Little Piggy
with my little piggies.

Thank you for lulling me to sleep with
"Puff the Magic Dragon" and "Twinkle,
Twinkle, Little Star."

Thank you for responding to my early-
morning cries in 5.3 seconds flat.

Thank you for holding a press
conference when I took my first steps.

Thank you for telling me I'd be okay
when I fell down and went "boom."

Thank you for hiding every boo-boo
behind a Band-Aid.®

*T*hank you for calling the doctor every time you discovered *any* symptom or had the faintest premonition something was wrong.

*T*hank you for taking my temperature despite my protests.

*T*hank you for keeping harmful things out of my reach.

Thank you for letting me sleep with my blankie and Pooh Bear.

Thank you for doing all the "right things" to raise me without the help of the talk show "experts."

Thank you for reading Dr. Seuss's *The Cat in the Hat* for nineteen straight nights.

Thank you for keeping your cool through my terrible twos, and my thoroughly exhausting threes, and my fearsome fours, and . . .

Thank you for not letting me be
"the death of you yet."

Thank you for tugging my thumb from
my mouth when it was time to stop
sucking my thumb.

Thank you for encouraging the artist in
me by sacrificing your walls to my
crayon masterpieces during
my Dada periods.

Thank you for tucking me in at night
and wishing me sweet dreams.

Thank you for promising not to let the
bedbugs bite.

Thank you for making me
say my prayers.

Thank you for pulling back your covers
for me to crawl under during
thunderstorms.

Thank you for teaching me right
from wrong.

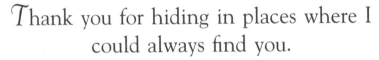

Thank you for hiding in places where I
could always find you.

Thank you for marking each quarter
inch I grew on the door frame.

Thank you for making me wash my hands after going to the bathroom.

Thank you for respecting my intelligence by not using the old Popeye bit to get me to eat my spinach.

Thank you for changing my sheets night after night until I learned to get to the bathroom in time.

Thank you for teaching me left from right.

Thank you for chasing me around with a tissue to wipe my nose so that I wouldn't use my sleeves.

Thank you for wiping my chocolate mustaches with your ever-present moist towelette.

*T*hank you for hiring battle-weary
baby-sitters who let me stay up
past my bedtime.

*T*hank you for licking your fingers to
pat down my cowlick.

*T*hank you for making me change my
underwear every day just in case I got
into an accident.

Thank you for my Fisher-Price
educational toys and for others that
were just plain fun.

Thank you for keeping my favorite ice
cream in the freezer.

Thank you for explaining the
significance of knocking on wood and
crossing my fingers.

Thank you for buying me cotton candy and chasing me through the maze of mirrors and riding in the front roller coaster car (even though you were scared and queasy).

Thank you for letting me ride my own horse on the merry-go-round.

Thank you for making me memorize my address and phone number.

Thank you for telling me that every line etched in Grandpa and Grammy's face was earned.

Thank you for cleaning my ears so that I wouldn't have hairy ears like Grandpa.

Thank you for making bath time fun time with a flotilla of ducks and battleships on a sea of bubbles.

Thank you for understanding that when I jumped on cracks I wasn't *really* trying to break your back.

*T*hank you for not letting me know what was going on behind your locked bedroom door.

*T*hank you for comforting me with the words "accidents do happen" after I broke something.

*T*hank you for dancing with me at weddings.

Thank you for not giving in to my
temper tantrums when I wanted
something in a store and you thought I
shouldn't have it.

Thank you for wheeling me around the
store in a shopping cart and for opening
a box of animal crackers even though
we hadn't paid for them yet.

Thank you for moderating the "Is not! Is too! Is not! Is too!" disputes.

Thank you for checking under the bed when I swore there was a monster there.

Thank you for not laughing at me, even when I asked Grammy if she was alive when they had dinosaurs.

*T*hank you for buying the cereal I loved
even if it had the most sugar and the
brightest colors.

*T*hank you for finding my Mr. Potato
Head parts when I lost them.

*T*hank you for holding my hand when
we walked down the street.

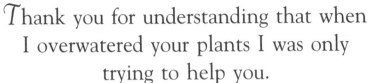

Thank you for understanding that when
I overwatered your plants I was only
trying to help you.

Thank you for giving me a penny for
the gumball machine.

Thank you for telling me to stop
snapping my gum and chewing
like a cow.

Thank you for saving a tabby cat from the animal shelter and allowing me to name her Dog Meat.

Thank you for saving the toilet paper rolls for my gerbils, Mickey and Minnie.

Thank you for buying me a new gerbil when Dog Meat found her way into the gerbil cage.

Thank you for understanding what I said when I spoke with my mouth full.

Thank you for encouraging me not to do it anymore.

Thank you for nagging me to take my vitamins so that I wouldn't get scurvy or rickets.

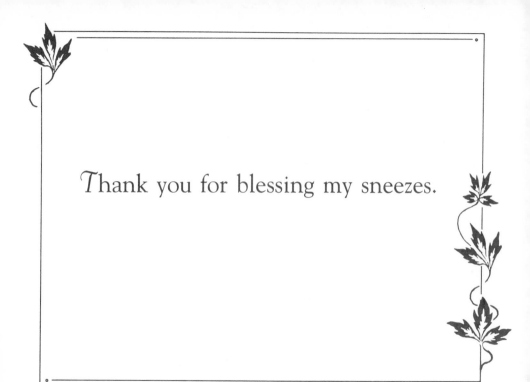

Thank you for blessing my sneezes.

Thank you for tucking my shirt into my pants and for tying my shoelaces before I tripped.

Thank you for cutting the bubble gum from my hair.

Thank you for telling all your friends that I was a child prodigy.

Thank you for saying "I don't care what so-and-so's mother said. I'm telling you this."

Thank you for holding firm and staying put, despite my attempts to convince you otherwise.

Thank you for cleaning my room after the tornado hit it.

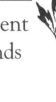

Thank you for playing a patient patient
while I dressed your imaginary wounds
in gauze and nearly turned you
into a mummy.

Thank you for reminding me about all
those starving children in far-off lands.

Thank you for not getting too mad
when I offered to ship my calf's liver
and brussels sprouts to those
starving children.

Thank you for scraping the dirt from under my fingernails and showing me how to do it myself.

Thank you for . . . Thank you for . . . Nah, the castor oil doesn't get a thank-you.

Thank you for asking "Who's there?" every time I said "Knock-knock."

Thank you for explaining that "cooties" were not really contagious.

Thank you for not getting too upset when you found your leftover tuna surprise casserole hidden in a napkin amid the dirty laundry at the bottom of the hamper.

Thank you for creating convincing excuses when I overheard you and Dad fighting.

Thank you for baking Toll House cookies and having a warm batch waiting for me with a tall glass of milk.

Thank you for saving me a spoonful of cookie dough.

Thank you for encouraging me to ask "Why? Why? Why? How come?"

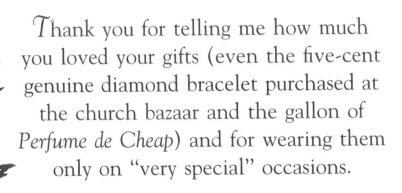

Thank you for taking me shopping (and paying) for Dad's Father's Day and birthday gifts.

Thank you for telling me how much you loved your gifts (even the five-cent genuine diamond bracelet purchased at the church bazaar and the gallon of *Perfume de Cheap*) and for wearing them only on "very special" occasions.

Thank you for catching me at the bottom of the slide.

Thank you for pushing me high enough on the swings to touch the clouds.

Thank you for teaching me to swim and to dive at the deep end of the pool.

Thank you for buying me a
Schwinn bike with a yellow banana
seat and wicked cool streamers
flowing from the handlebars.

Thank you for holding on to my bicycle seat and running at my side for six whole blocks the day you took off my training wheels.

Thank you for disinfecting my scraped knee and kissing the wound to make it feel better.

Thank you for promising me that time healed all wounds (unless I picked off the scabs).

Thank you for letting me cling to your back, with my nails digging into your sunburned skin, when I thought I saw a fin in the ocean.

Thank you for taking me back-to-school shopping for a three-ring binder and pencil case.

Thank you for prying me from your leg and forcing me to attend my first day of school.

Thank you for calling "Rise and shine" so that I would always get to school on time.

Thank you for finding all of the things that I misplaced so that I wouldn't miss the bus.

Thank you for not letting me leave the house dressed "like that"— most of the time.

Thank you for framing my art class creations and hanging them around the house.

Thank you for drawing the multiplication flash cards and drilling me on the seven-times table until I knew it perfectly.

Thank you for showing off my gold-starred spelling tests on the refrigerator door.

Thank you for being a great Mama Bear and protecting your cub by calling Mrs. Dudley to tell her that her little "Milk Dud" was stealing my lunch money.

Thank you for letting me play hooky from school the time you knew that I had held the thermometer to the light to make it read 109 degrees.

Thank you for allowing me to eat school cafeteria meals on pizza days and for filling my lunch box with Fluffernutter sandwiches on fish days.

Thank you for making me wear glasses despite my protests so that I could see the blackboard.

Thank you for attending Parent-Teacher Nights and telling me all the good things my teachers had to say.

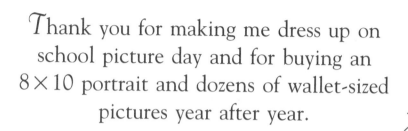

$\mathcal{T}$hank you for making me dress up on school picture day and for buying an 8×10 portrait and dozens of wallet-sized pictures year after year.

$\mathcal{T}$hank you for understanding "new math" and helping me with my homework.

Thank you for cheering my performance
as a street urchin in Mrs. Marshall's
3rd-grade production of *Oliver*.

Thank you for making burlap costumes
for all the orphans.

Thank you for whispering my only line
from the audience to jog my memory.

Thank you for insisting that I would
have made a better Oliver.

Thank you for celebrating my report card "Excellents" and helping me work on my "Needs Improvements."

Thank you for eating the "mystery" dinner that I cooked for you.

Thank you for showing me that my half-empty glass was really half-full.

Thank you for your wonderful smiles.

Thank you for not looking under the
bed after I cleaned my bedroom.

Thank you for dressing up like a witch
on Halloween and trying to scare
my friends.

Thank you for giving out the best
Halloween treats on the block.

Thank you for checking my candy
when I returned home to make sure
it was safe.

Thank you for cooking the greatest
Thanksgiving feasts.

Thank you for teaching me
to give thanks.

Thank you for wrapping me up in twelve layers of clothes underneath my snowsuit so that I resembled the Pillsbury Doughboy.

Thank you for unwrapping my layers of clothes and holding me upside down to pull off my rubber boots twenty minutes later so I could go to the bathroom.

Thank you for making snow angels with me in the front yard after a snowfall.

Thank you for letting me use your favorite scarf to keep my five-foot snowman warm.

Thank you for teaching me it was okay to fall off my ice skates as long as I got up and tried again.

Thank you for creating magic
during the holidays.

Thank you for humoring my urgent
pleas for every toy featured
in the *Sears Wish Book*.

Thank you for not believing me when I
sang "All I want for Christmas is my
two front teeth."

Thank you for letting me help select
the Christmas tree.

Thank you for wrapping my presents so that I couldn't tell what was inside—no matter how hard I shook them.

Thank you for watching *Rudolph the Red-Nosed Reindeer*, *Frosty the Snowman*, *The Grinch Who Stole Christmas*, and all of the other holiday specials with me.

Thank you for letting me light the holiday candles that made our living room glow.

Thank you for answering the letters that I mailed to the North Pole.

Thank you for baking terrific Christmas cookies and letting me decorate them with you.

Thank you for staring with me for
hours into the dark Christmas Eve sky
searching for Santa's sleigh.

Thank you for filling our stockings and
hanging them by the chimney
with care.

Thank you for not putting coal in my
stocking despite your warnings that I
might deserve it.

Thank you for wrapping up my puppy, Toto, and placing the wiggling box under the tree.

Thank you for filling a bowl with my dinner, placing it on the floor, and letting me eat with my puppy.

Thank you for letting Toto curl up with me on my bed.

Thank you for feeding Dog Meat and Toto—all the times that I forgot.

Thank you for being my tooth fairy (and keeping up with inflation).

Thank you for being my Valentine.

Thank you for hiding chocolate eggs and marshmallow bunnies for the Easter morning egg hunt.

Thank you for not washing out my mouth with soap despite the threats.

Thank you for doing things for my "own good."

Thank you for telling me about the day I was born.

Thank you for giving me real orange juice instead of that gritty orange sludge that the astronauts drank.

Thank you for letting me run away
from home and hide under the front
porch for an hour.

Thank you for walking out on the
porch (pretending to not know where I
was hiding) and crying loud enough for
me to hear I was missed.

Thank you for welcoming me
back home.

Thank you for never running away
from home—no matter how
tempted *you* were.

Thank you for not picketing *too* long when you went on strike until the family pitched in around the house.

Thank you for following me to my friend's house and hiding behind trees, to make sure that I arrived safely and that I went to where I said I was going.

Thank you for explaining to me that
trust has to be earned.

Thank you for trusting me.

Thank you for making me feel good by
regularly complimenting me.

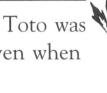

Thank you for telling me that Toto was safe and happy in Doggy Heaven when she passed away.

Thank you for insisting that beauty is in the eye of the beholder . . . and reassuring me that what you were beholding was beautiful.

Thank you for selling my candy bars at your office so that my school could purchase audiovisual equipment.

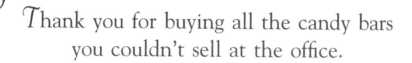

Thank you for buying all the candy bars you couldn't sell at the office.

Thank you for letting me decorate my bedroom walls with magazine pictures and posters of my favorite singers and TV stars.

Thank you for not being a "Mommie Dearest."

Thank you for telling me "One day you'll thank me for this." Today's the day. . . . Thank you for that.

Thank you for showing me how to use
public toilets without touching
the toilet seat.

Thank you for surrounding me with
unconditional love.

Thank you for not making me a
child star.

Thank you for answering me when
I asked you every day
"What's for dinner?"

Thank you for holding my hand as they
wheeled my gurney toward
the operating room.

Thank you for having the doctor save
my tonsils so that I could keep them in
a jar after the operation.

Thank you for teaching me to think
before I act.

Thank you for reminding me to turn off
the lights and to stop the faucet from
dripping and to jiggle the toilet
handle. . . .

Thank you for saying nice things about
me when I was within earshot.

Thank you for showing me how
Slinkies can walk down the stairs.

*T*hank you for asking what was wrong
whenever I cried.

*T*hank you for stopping Grammy from
putting a bowl on my head to
cut my hair.

*T*hank you for making a giant bowl of
popcorn with melted butter just as my
favorite TV show started.

Thank you for signing me up for a library card.

Thank you for paying my overdue fees even though last time you said it would be your last time.

Thank you for teaching me to respect all of God's creatures, great and small, except for cockroaches.

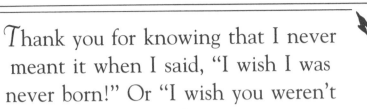

Thank you for knowing that I never meant it when I said, "I wish I was never born!" Or "I wish you weren't my mother!"

Thank you for making me wait half an hour for my food to digest before I went swimming.

Thank you for making sure I brushed my teeth every night and had a dental checkup every six months.

Thank you for laying tracks on my teeth to straighten them out.

Thank you for distracting me before the doctor gave me shots.

Thank you for asking the doctor to give me a lollipop.

Thank you for being Dr. Mom and taking care of me even when you were sick.

Thank you for rubbing my chest with VapoRub and checking me all night long when I had "that flu."

Thank you for giving me the "*mmm mmm good*" Campbell's Chicken Noodle Soup.

Thank you for teaching me that an apple a day keeps the doctor away (and washing it really well first).

Thank you for not charging me a penny every time I said "ain't."

Thank you for letting me keep a snake in my bedroom.

$\mathcal{T}$hank you for reminding me that my
boredom was my fault and could be
corrected by my imagination
and creativity.

$\mathcal{T}$hank you for explaining what
do-si-do means.

$\mathcal{T}$hank you for teaching me to be
generous by dropping your spare change
into other people's cups.

Thank you for leaving the onions out of the spaghetti sauce that you served me and making a separate sauce for the others.

Thank you for piling real whipped cream on top of the raspberry 1-2-3 Jell-O.

Thank you for never serving "mystery meat" for dinner.

Thank you for your kind words when they were needed the most.

Thank you for always being my friend.

Thank you for laughing with me.

Thank you for crying with me.

Thank you for your big hugs
and kisses.

Thank you for wishing and wanting only the best for me.

Thank you for not making me kiss Aunt Gertrude when she wanted a big wet one.

Thank you for teaching me to leave other people's belongings just as I had found them—except for the neighbor's flowers that I had picked for you.

Thank you for keeping your promises
and expecting me to do the same.

Thank you for using the candlesnuffer
that I made for you in shop class.

Thank you for encouraging me to walk
in someone else's shoes before I criticize.

Thank you for letting me beat you in
checkers, Monopoly, Scrabble,
Parcheesi, Life, Crazy Eights,
and Go Fish.

Thank you for humoring me while
I gloated.

Thank you for teaching me about the birds and the bees.

Thank you for hiding *The Joy of Sex* where I could find it to help me fill in some of the details you left out.

Thank you for not calling me stupid or dummy or idiot, and especially for never swearing at me.

Thank you for saying "I love you."

Thank you for sharing the joys of chocolate with me.

Thank you for making time for those long talks about anything and everything.

Thank you for telling me there was a time and place for everything.

Thank you for making me pick up my clothes from the floor and put them where they belonged. (Where did you say it was?)

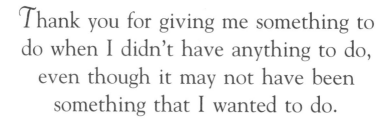

Thank you for giving me something to do when I didn't have anything to do, even though it may not have been something that I wanted to do.

Thank you for requiring me to wash the dishes and make my bed and mow the lawn and shovel the walkways and driveways and . . .

Thank you for my first name. I always liked it.

Thank you for reminding me that it will all come out in the wash (except for the socks the washing machine ate).

Thank you for singing that the sun would come out "Tomorrow" on my darkest days.

Thank you for telling me "Ask your father" when you didn't want to say no, thus increasing my odds for success.

*T*hank you for always giving me your
very best and expecting the same
in return.

*T*hank you for showing me how to
appreciate the beauty that
life has to offer.

*T*hank you for welcoming my friends to
our home.

Thank you for refereeing the family
squabbles and skirmishes.

Thank you for not showing favoritism.
(Even though I know you
liked me best!)

Thank you for sharing your doubts and
insecurities with me.

Thank you for taking me and my friends to my favorite restaurant on my birthdays and for having the waitresses embarrass me by singing "Happy Birthday" off-key—even though I had begged you not to.

Thank you for my home-baked birthday cakes with the trick candles that can't be blown out.

Thank you for inspiring me to follow my dreams.

Thank you for taking me with you on vacations.

Thank you for making my posters when I ran for a class office.

Thank you for consoling me after the election didn't work out.

Thank you for working days, and sometimes nights, to put food on the table and a roof over my head and clothes on my back.

Thank you for putting up with my teenage mood swings.

Thank you for tolerating me during my fifties phase.

Thank you for tolerating me during my disco phase.

Thank you for tolerating me during my "everybody's doing it" phase.

Thank you for tolerating me during my ripped Levi's phase (and for not making me pay you back when I deliberately ripped my new Levi's).

Thank you for smiling through my sarcastic phase.

Thank you for understanding my "geez, you're embarrassing me" phase.

Thank you for making me sit before you and smoke an entire pack of cigarettes—watching me inhale every drag and turn green—after you caught me smoking.

Thank you for letting me know how much I had hurt you when you caught me in a lie.

Thank you for trusting me again.

Thank you for not quitting on me.

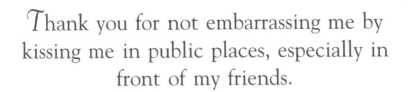

Thank you for not embarrassing me by kissing me in public places, especially in front of my friends.

Thank you for mumbling back when I mumbled in order to prove a point.

Thank you for not asking the cable company to disconnect my MTV.

Thank you for insisting on seeing my report card.

Thank you for rewarding my As and Bs with praise.

Thank you for rewarding my Cs with "You can do better."

Thank you for rewarding my Ds and Fs with "You #$%& well better do better!"

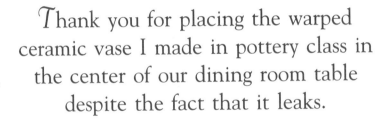

Thank you for typing my school reports
and papers and then teaching me to
type them myself.

Thank you for placing the warped
ceramic vase I made in pottery class in
the center of our dining room table
despite the fact that it leaks.

Thank you for showing me how to
blow-dry my hair.

Thank you for subscribing to my favorite magazines.

Thank you for letting me wear the brand of jeans that everyone else was wearing.

Thank you for reminding me that I don't have to jump off a bridge just because everyone else is doing it.

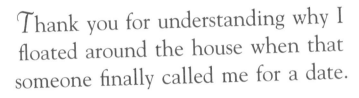

Thank you for letting me cry on your shoulder when that certain someone—the biggest jerk in the whole universe—didn't notice me.

Thank you for understanding why I floated around the house when that someone finally called me for a date.

Thank you for comforting me after the demise of my first "love" when the first date failed to produce a second date.

Thank you for letting me cry on your shoulder when another certain someone—the biggest jerk in the whole universe—didn't notice me.

Thank you for understanding why I floated around the house when *that* someone finally called me for a date.

Thank you for comforting me after the first date with my new "love" failed to produce a second date.

*T*hank you for letting me cry on your shoulder when still *another* certain someone—the biggest jerk in the whole universe—didn't notice me.

*T*hank you for understanding why I floated around the house when *that* someone finally called me for a date.

*T*hank you for comforting me after the first date failed to produce a second date—*again*.

Thank you for telling me about all the other fish in the sea.

Thank you for warning me about the "H" bomb—hormones.

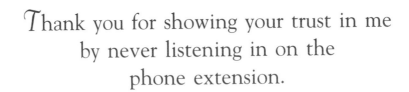

Thank you for showing your trust in me
by never listening in on the
phone extension.

Thank you for helping me find a cure
for my acne.

Thank you for expecting me to voice
my opinions.

Thank you for swallowing your I-told-you-so's when you were so tempted.

Thank you for taking 1,987,321 telephone messages for me.

Thank you for helping me get my driver's license by letting me practice with you in the car.

Thank you for trusting me to drive the
family car alone.

Thank you for warning me, constantly,
about the hazards of drinking and
driving so that I could live long enough
to thank you.

Thank you for warning me
about hitchhiking.

Thank you for loaning me money to pay my parking tickets.

Thank you for showing me why my vote is important.

Thank you for explaining why jealousy is a misguided emotion.

Thank you for not telling Dad about
you-know-what.

Thank you for staying up late into the
night waiting for me to return home.

Thank you for being a "SuperMom"
and for doing all that you do.

Thank you for not saying, after reading the last entry, "Okay, what do you want now?"

Thank you for demonstrating how to appreciate the beauty in the beast.

Thank you for calling me when you were late so that I didn't worry. (I'm sorry for those times when I forgot to call, and I'm sorry that you had to worry.)

Thank you for looking so beautiful at my high school graduation.

Thank you for my special high school
graduation gift.

Thank you for cooking 18,983 meals
(and still counting).

Thank you for preparing me for college.

Thank you for promising to keep the
empty nest warm in case
I got homesick.

Thank you for taking care of my cat,
Dog Meat the Fourth, while I was away.

Thank you for not hiding your tears
and for telling me that you'd miss me.

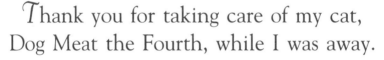

Thank you for scrimping on the household budget for many, many years to pay my college tuition.

Thank you for attending Parents' Weekends and taking some of my friends out to dinner.

Thank you for forwarding my mail to me.

Thank you for not closing the door in
my face when I brought home three
months' worth of laundry.

Thank you for always cooking my
favorite dinner when I came home
for visits.

Thank you for keeping my room just
the way it was—well, maybe just
a little cleaner.

Thank you for visiting me when homesickness reared its ugly head.

Thank you for mailing goody-laden care packages to me.

Thank you for your unexpected phone calls.

Thank you for sending me flowers to
cheer me up when I was down.

Thank you for realizing that I needed
"space" to "find" myself.

Thank you for letting me spread my
wings to fly—even though I flew into a
tree or two.

Thank you for helping me write my résumé when it was time to leave college and confront the real world.

Thank you for attending my college graduation.

Thank you for not throwing out my stuff the day I left for college.

Thank you for understanding that the hours spent commuting each day make it difficult for me to call home as often as I'd like.

Thank you for forgiving me when I missed that Valentine's Day at the end of an eighty-hour workweek—even though that was no excuse.

Thank you for missing me so much
but letting me go.

Thank you for having a family portrait taken.

Thank you for my green thumb.

Thank you for warning me to wash the tops of the cans and bang them on both top and bottom before opening them.

Thank you for giving me your best recipes so I could inherit your great cooking talent.

Thank you for teaching me why it's important to eat healthy foods.

Thank you for reminding me to check my body for signs of disease.

Thank you for teaching me that you never have a second chance to make a great first impression.

Thank you for encouraging me to reach for my goals.

Thank you for not asking me (too many times) "When are you getting married?"

Thank you for introducing me to the people at Goodwill and for showing me how my seldom-used possessions can benefit others.

Thank you for almost never lying to me—well, except for the one or two little fibs that I will remember when I have kids.

Thank you for my common sense.

Thank you for clipping out articles that
would encourage me to keep learning.

Thank you for showing me how to be
thrifty and get value for my money.

Thank you for reminding me that
overnight mail was the last resort for
the unprepared—until the fax
came along.

Thank you for telling me that just as
many "hers" live on the planet
as "hims."

Thank you for teaching me how to
squeeze a cantaloupe and to find
a ripe avocado.

Thank you for the surprise gifts and
notes in the mail.

Thank you for showing me that what I
have to give to someone might be
worth more than I dare think.

Thank you for saying "Hang in there"
when life took me on
a high-speed chase.

Thank you for teaching me the
Twenty-third Psalm.

*T*hank you for letting me know that no matter what, I am always welcome back home.

*T*hank you for instilling in me a strong sense of self-reliance.

*T*hank you for still keeping pictures of me all over your home.

Thank you for creating a video
from your old Super 8 movies with
the songs "Memories" and "You
Light Up My Life"
playing throughout.

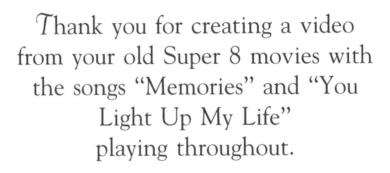

Thank you for teaching me to respect people who are different from me and to appreciate those differences.

Thank you for showing me that with education no doors are locked.

Thank you for teaching me "to thine own self be true."

Thank you for always being there when
I needed you.

Thank you for giving me a healthy dose
of skepticism when confronted with
claims from advertisers, politicians,
lawyers, and car salespeople.

Thank you for not being impressed with
people who are all fluff
without substance.

Thank you for telling me all your best homespun clichés (the ones I thought you had created before I read one of those best-selling little books about life and such), like . . .

. . . *Unless you paddle your own canoe, you won't move.*

. . . *When life gives you lemons, make lemonade.*

. . . *No pain, no strain, no gain.*

Thank you for cultivating my sense
of humor.

Thank you for insisting that I write
thank-you notes the very next day.

Thank you for reminding me that my
self-worth was not dependent on others.

Thank you for teaching me
about my roots.

Thank you for stressing that it is important to strive for my goals.

Thank you for teaching me that life does not come with money-back guarantees and warranties.

Thank you for showing me how to find opportunities in the problems I face.

Thank you for explaining that only a few experts exist and that those who profess to be ought to be regarded with suspicion, and that includes my father.

Thank you for reminding me not to judge a book by its cover.

Thank you for encouraging me to live my own dreams rather than someone else's.

Thank you for all of your advice, even though you probably thought it went in one ear, ricocheted off the walls like a rubber Super Ball, and bounced out the other ear.

Thank you for teaching me that nothing ever comes easy and that you have to work *very hard* to realize your goals.

Thank you for grounding me with a
strong sense of reality.

Thank you for sharing with me the
mistakes that you made so that I can try
to avoid them.

Thank you for living by
the Ten Commandments.

Thank you for showing me how to thank God.

Thank you for defining altruism, integrity, perseverance, and loyalty by your example.

Thank you for our "family values."

Thank you for being my hero.

Thank you for passing on to me our family's greatest and most valuable asset . . . our reputation.

Thank you for a great childhood.

Thank you for preparing me
for adulthood.

Thank you for giving me
the best years of your life.

Thank you for your sacrifices.

Thank you for showing me how to express my love.

Thank you for being you.

Thank you for teaching me to say thank you.

Thank you for all of the times that I failed to say thank you.

Thank you for your love.

Thank you with all of my heart and soul.

Thank you for being mine.

And most of all, thank you for
being the best Mom
in the universe!

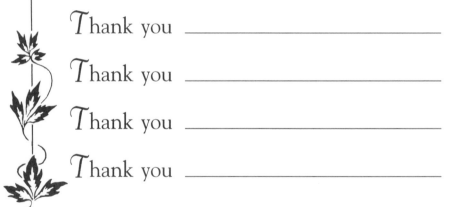

Special Thank-Yous Just for My Mom

*T*hank you _____

*T*hank you _____

*T*hank you _____

*T*hank you _____

Thank you _____

Thank you _____

Thank you _____

Thank you _____

Thank you _____

ABOUT THE AUTHORS

Scott is the son of Glenn and Gail Matthews.
Tamara is the daughter of Charles and Odeline
Townes and Alexander Nikuradse.

If you have a special thank-you for your Mom that you'd like to share, please send it to:

Scott Matthews and Tamara Nikuradse
Bantam Books
1540 Broadway
New York, NY 10036

Please include your name and address so that we can give you credit if we include it in future editions.
Thank you.

DON'T FORGET DAD!

Dear Dad,

- Thank you for not dropping me on my head when I was little.
- Thank you for pulling the worms out of my mouth when we went fishing.
- Thank you for never dropping me off at the orphanage or selling me to the circus.
- Thank you for staying up half the night on Christmas Eve trying to translate the unreadable instructions and assemble my toys before I woke up at five in the morning and dragged you out of bed.

Dear Dad, Thank You for Being Mine—
ask for it at your local bookstore.